Wonderlands by the Waves

A History of the Seaside Resorts of Lancashire

by John K. Walton

Lancashire County Books, 1992

Wonderlands by the Waves: A History of the Seaside Resorts of Lancashire

by John K. Walton

Published by Lancashire County Books, 143 Corporation St., Preston, in association with the Lancaster Branch of the Historical Association

The Historical Association (founded in 1906) is a national organisation with branches throughout the country. It provides a range of activities and publications for people who share an interest in, and love for, the past. Further details can be obtained from Historical Association, 59a Kennington Park Road, London SE11 4JH

First edition, 1992

Typeset and designed by Carnegie Publishing, 18 Maynard St., Preston
Printed and bound in the UK by T. Snape & Co., Preston

British Library Cataloguing-in-Publication Data
A CIP catalogue record for this book is available from the British Library

ISBN 1-871236-19-3

Contents

A group of holidaymakers paddling in the sea at Blackpool

Wonderlands by the Waves

T HE history of the seaside is often assumed to be trivial and
not worth examining. It is difficult to reconcile this attitude
with the knowledge that seaside tourism is now big business
world-wide, generating profits and problems and providing plenty
of work for academic economists, geographers and planners. And
if we look for the historical roots of this phenomenon, we find an
enthralling story, with plenty of messages, direct or indirect, for
the present day. Within this history, the seaside resorts of Lancashire play a unique and pioneering part.

THE SEASIDE HOLIDAY, and the seaside resort as a distinctive kind
of town, are in their modern guise effectively English inventions.
They originated in the craze for medicinal
sea-bathing which began in the mid-eight-
eenth century, and (like the earlier and over-   *The Origins And*
lapping fashion for spa waters) soon spread
from the aristocracy and landed gentry to the   *Influence of the English*
prospering middle ranks of an emergent
industrial society. The leading early resorts   *Seaside Resort*
were in the south-east, close to the wealth
and high fashion of London. Margate and
Brighton were the pioneers, although royal patronage helped
Brighton to outdistance its rivals from the 1780s onwards. By this
time, motives of fashion and amusement were at least as important

From the earliest days of the seaside holiday, the beach was given over to children and donkeys as well as bathing-machines, shell-hunters and seaweed-collectors. Lytham specialised in the kind of respectable middle-class holiday in which children were at the centre of the stage. Working-class visitors found it very difficult to afford holidays when the children were small.

as health in luring people to the seaside, and smaller resorts were sprouting on all the coastlines of provincial England, catering mainly for local and less affluent markets. Developments in Scotland and Ireland came a little later, but in England the seaside holiday industry was already growing rapidly by the turn of the century. At this point the fashion was already spreading in Western Europe, especially France and Germany, and it was soon to take root in northern Spain. Ultimately the seaside holiday was to be nearly as universal a cultural export as association football. It spread throughout the English-speaking world, from the United States to South Africa and Australia. In South America its development was influenced by Spanish as well as English practices, just as (for example) sea-bathing in Tunisia in the inter-war years may have had separate local roots as well as French colonial encouragement; but almost everywhere the rise of the seaside resort can be traced to English origins, whether directly or at one remove. Admittedly, more recent developments embrace the sun-bathing fashion which originated in the Edwardian years and owes more to the French Riviera than to England; but the association of the seaside with the pursuit of health, pleasure and holiday was long established before this new dimension was added, and the fact remains that the seaside holiday as we know it originated in the England of the Industrial Revolution.

Seaside resorts were not just an English invention: they also grew faster and further in the England of the nineteenth century, and produced a uniquely extravagant variety of sub-species to cater for different classes and tastes. Already in 1851 the Census Report found that eleven seaside resorts constituted the fastest-growing type of town during half a century of unprecedented urban and industrial growth; and although this statistic was misleading, because it was based on the percentage growth-rate for towns which were very small to begin with, it cannot be discounted. As resorts continued to increase and multiply, in 1881 the total population of 106 seaside resorts in England and Wales reached about one million, and in 1911 seaside resorts accounted for about one resident in every 22. Their actual influence was much greater than this, because not only did immense numbers of people spend anything from a day to a month as seaside visitors each year, but also migration flows in and out of seaside resorts were particularly heavy, so that an impressive proportion of the population could expect to spend part of their lives as seaside residents.

LANCASHIRE's seaside resorts became particularly numerous, populous and important, especially after the railway system began to develop in earnest during the 1840s. Blackpool and Southport were already beginning to stir in the later eighteenth century, and Lytham and Morecambe were not far behind; but at the 1851 census only Southport made much of a showing, with a population of 8,694 making it the tenth largest British seaside resort. Lytham, with 2,698 inhabitants, and Blackpool, with 2,564, were a long way down the list, while Morecambe, with only 1,301 residents, was not even in the top fifty. After this, however, development was rapid. In 1881 Southport was the fifth largest British resort, with over 33,000 inhabitants, and Blackpool was twentieth, with nearly 13,000. Lytham and Morecambe lagged a long way behind, although Morecambe was one of

The Growth of the Lancashire Resorts

The core of Morecambe's mid-Victorian sea-front development, seen in 1918 with shops and sea-front dining rooms to cater for the trippers.

The carefully-planned urban layout of the new resort of St Annes which offered quiet family holidays for the comfortably-off, within easy reach of the fleshpots of Blackpool

the twenty fastest-growing resorts in these mid-Victorian years, while Blackpool was fifth fastest (if we measure growth in percentage terms) and Southport ninth. But the next thirty years saw the most spectacular developments. Blackpool overtook Southport to become, in 1911, Britain's fifth largest resort, with over 58,000 inhabitants at an April census. Southport was ninth, with just over 50,000, although if Birkdale, next door, had been included it would have had 70,000 people, moving it into third place behind Brighton and Bournemouth. Meanwhile Morecambe had over 12,000 residents and Lytham nearly 10,000, on a par with nearby St Annes, a new speculation which had only just started to emerge from the sandhills in 1881. If we add in the new developments at Bispham and Cleveleys on the Fylde coast north of Blackpool, and the little resorts of Morecambe Bay, especially Arnside and Grange-over-Sands, the picture is even more remarkable.

The county's seaside resorts housed about 160,000 people, about 1 in 30 of the population of a part of England known mainly for its enormous sprawl of smoky manufacturing and mining towns, and for the great cities of Manchester and Liverpool. As this evidence makes clear, Lancashire also contained one of the most populous seaside resort systems in the world, matched only by the Sussex coast and by the French Riviera. Nothing else was on this scale, or anywhere near it. On the Fylde, in particular, there was already very little undeveloped coastline. And within this mass of seaside bricks and mortar lay the unique experience of Blackpool, the world's first working-class seaside resort, which was propelled mainly by demand from industrial workers to become, in sheer weight of numbers, the third fastest-growing resort in Britain between 1881 and 1911.

In world terms this was early growth, although within Britain the south-east coast had taken the lead, especially Sussex and Kent. But the pattern of Lancashire's resort development had already been firmly laid out by the eve of the First World War: Blackpool with its exuberant and unique working-class heart; Morecambe catering mainly for a more respectable stratum of foremen and clerical workers, and with a distinctive Yorkshire bias to its catchment area; Southport cultivating a more sedate and up-market image, with wealthy residents and commuters forming an increasingly important part of its population; Lytham and St Annes following a similar path, though with less ostentation; and the smaller resorts of Morecambe Bay offering scenic and climatic advantages to a comfortably-off public which appreciated the proximity of the

*Between 1905 and 1933 Morecambe's attractions included the
opportunity to watch famous ships being dismantled at T. W. Ward's
breaker's yard in the old harbour. Ward's activities would have appealed
to skilled industrial workers, and they add interest to this beach scene of
the 1920s, when Morecambe had not yet abandoned the traditional
bathing-machine.*

Lake District. This was not the end of the matter, however. The
Lancashire resorts continued to flourish, despite growing competition from various kinds of rival, and in the face of enduring
economic depression in much of industrial Lancashire between
the wars. The 1921 census was taken in June, but it is still arresting to find Blackpool, swollen by boundary changes as well as
summer residents and early visitors, topping the 100,000 mark,
while Morecambe, which had also extended its territory, had
doubled to more than 24,000. Significantly, perhaps, whereas
Southport had set the pace for most of the nineteenth century, the
more up-market resorts were now growing more slowly; and this
pattern was to continue in subsequent years.

The 1920s saw little growth in population terms in the resorts, and
Lancashire as a whole was now stagnating, as its older industries

*Southport's open-air seawater bathing pool was an enormous success in
the inter-war years, when there was growing emphasis on physical
display and sunbathing. In 1928 more than 465,000 people were admitted
as bathers and spectators.*

fell on hard times. But growth resumed in earnest in Blackpool in
the 1930s, which were prosperous times in the resort's holiday
economy as it gained from the increased spending power of those
who were in work, especially in the Midlands manufacturing districts which were part of its catchment area for visitors. Morecambe grew even faster than Blackpool in percentage terms
between 1931 and 1951, at which point it had more than 37,000
inhabitants, while Blackpool was close to the top of the international league with four times as many. Southport, Lytham St Annes
and the classier small resorts continued to grow more slowly, perhaps because Blackpool and Morecambe were themselves
attracting commuters and retired people in significant numbers as
well as taking the lion's share of holiday expansion, which was
fuelled by the belated advent of paid holidays in the cotton industry
on the eve of the Second World War.

Lancashire's seaside resorts had continued to expand while
most of the county faltered and declined. Between 1931 and 1951
Blackpool and Southport were the county's fastest-growing large
towns, while Morecambe was prominent among the mainly subur-
ban settlements which set the pace lower down the urban league
table, along with the Blackpool offshoots (as they were becoming)
of Poulton-le-Fylde and Thornton-Cleveleys. By 1951 seaside
resorts accounted for about 1 in 16 of Lancashire's population; and
this does not include the northern suburbs of Liverpool which
stretched out towards Southport along the shoreline. Growth in the
resorts proper did tail off in the 1950s and 1960s, despite an 'Indian
Summer' of prosperity in the traditional holiday industry before
the full dawning of the age of the motorway, the jet plane and the
package tour; but by that time Lancashire's seaside had had a
longer innings in the forefront of resort growth and enterprise in an
international context than had the county's more famous cotton
industry.

TO EXPLAIN this remarkable phenomenon, we need to go back to
the beginnings of Lancashire's seaside resorts, to trace the changing social realities which underlie the popu-
lation figures. We also need to bear in mind
The Sea and that the rise of the Lancashire resorts was
achieved without the added attractions of
Sea-bathing alluring scenery (except for the Morecambe
Bay resorts, which grew relatively slowly
and belatedly), historical interest, quaintness
or climatic advantages, Southport's attempts to portray itself as
the Montpellier of England notwithstanding. What counted here
was the sea itself, ease of access, and above all, from an early
stage, artificial attractions and careful municipal management.
    The origins of sea-bathing in Lancashire combined elements of
the 'polite culture' of the aristocracy, gentry, merchants and profes-
sionals who enabled the seaside holiday to become a commercial
proposition, and the 'popular culture' of the lower orders, of custom, magic and the oral tradition. On the one hand, by the late
eighteenth century Blackpool and Southport were already receiv-
ing August visitors in their hundreds, drawn from the middle ranks
of Lancashire society, with a few intrepid visitors from Halifax or
even distant Birmingham. As the Birmingham bookseller William
Hutton and his daughter Catherine remarked, these were very

Sea Bathing.

The Public are respectfully informed that an OMNIBUS called

THE SAFETY

Will commence Running to the SIMPSON'S HOTEL,

BLACKPOOL,

On Wednesday, the 21st May, 1845,

From the HOLE IN THE WALL INN, in COLNE,

And from the OLD RED LION INN, BURNLEY,

Through Blackburn, Preston, and Lytham to Blackpool Three Times a Week, viz:—

On Wednesdays and Fridays from Colne, starting at Six o'clock in the Morning, and leaving Burnley at Seven o'clock, and reaching Blackpool at Two o'clock in the Afternoon, and on Monday Mornings from Burnley at Seven o'clock.

The above Omnibus will leave Blackpool returning to the above places every Tuesday, Thursday, and Saturday, at Ten o'clock in the Forenoon.

N. B. Arrangements will be made so that Passengers will be able to proceed through to Blackpool, without stopping except for change of Horses.

PERFORMED BY THE PUBLIC'S MOST OBEDIENT SERVANTS,

STUTTARD, ALLEN, & Co.

H. EARNSHAW, PRINTER, COLNE.

Stage-coach services to Blackpool from towns as distant as Halifax were already operating in the 1780s; but this advertisement from 1845 was to be one of the last, as railway extensions made the older and more expensive form of transport obsolete.

Courtesy of Lancashire Record Office, DDBd 57/5/2

provincial, unpretentious people, and their table manners left
something to be desired. But they were drawn to the seaside as fol-
lowers of the new medical fashion for sea-bathing in high society, and
their presence was lucrative enough to stimulate the development of
hotels and stage-coach services. The cream of Lancashire, as of northern society generally, still went to more fashionable places, whether
that meant Harrogate, Buxton, Scarborough or the southern resorts;
but enough Bolton manufacturers and Manchester lawyers were left
to launch sea-bathing villages where hitherto there had been nothing but sand-dunes and fishermen's cottages.

    Alongside this pattern of early development, which was com-
mon to much of the English seaside, was something much older,
stranger and more distinctive. It was a well-established custom of
popular sea-bathing, associated not with the fashionable writings
of formally qualified doctors but with the belief that at the August
spring tide there was 'physic in the sea' which would wash away
the impurities of the year and protect against illness in the months
to come. This belief brought weavers, cottagers and artisans to the
coast from as far away as the Burnley and Manchester areas, to
drink sea-water by the gallon (with the help of generous measures
of spirits to fortify the stomach) and to bathe. This calendar custom
was popular all along the Lancashire coast, from Liverpool to
Southport to Preston (where the River Ribble is tidal) to Lytham,
Blackpool and Hest Bank, north of Morecambe. It is not unique to
Lancashire, nor even to the British Isles: parallels can be found at
Aberystwyth, in the Severn estuary above Bristol, and most
remarkably of all, at Biarritz in south-west France, where the Bas-
ques in the early and mid-nineteenth century processed down to the
sea to bathe and dance at the same time of year. Whatever its
origins and associations, the 'Bathing Sunday' tradition, as it was
called, was increasing in observance and popularity in the early
nineteenth century, and by the 1820s enormous cavalcades of
horses and conveyances passed through Preston on their way to the
coast. In the early railway age these unpretentious bathers transferred themselves to the cheap trains, making the second week in
August the busiest part of the Blackpool season. This tradition ensured that working people from inland Lancashire had an established belief in the healthiness and pleasurable associations of
sea-bathing which might have been reinforced by fashion and
orthodox medicine, but had its own distinctive traditional origins.

    At this stage, however, it was the middle and upper classes
whose spending power and extended visits conjured up resort

LANCASHIRE & YORKSHIRE
RAILWAY.

SEA BATHING
FOR THE
WORKING CLASSES.

ON AND AFTER SUNDAY MORNING NEXT,
and on each succeeding Sunday until further notice, with a view of
affording the benefit of

SEA BATHING,
A Train will leave the following Stations for
FLEETWOOD AND BLACKPOOL.

FARES
THERE AND BACK THE SAME DAY.

	A.M.	Males.	Females & Children.
Leave Manchester at	6 0	3s. 0d.	1s. 6d.
,, Bolton at	6 30	2s. 6d.	1s. 3d.
,, Chorley at	7 10	2s. 0d.	1s. 0d.
,, Preston at	7 40	2s. 0d.	1s. 0d.

Arriving at Fleetwood at 9 a.m.

FROM SALFORD STATION.

MANCHESTER TO LIVERPOOL
FARES there and back same day.

	Males.	Females and Children.
At 7 a.m.	2s. 6d.	1s. 6d.

BURY TO LIVERPOOL, BLACKPOOL,
AND FLEETWOOD.
FARES there and back same day.

	Males.	Female
	2s. 6d.	

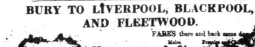

*A timetable hand-bill for the controversial Sunday
excursions of the late 1840s. Care was taken to ensure
that the working-class bathers would be able to attend
church, although it is unlikely that many did so.*

Courtesy of Lancashire Record Office, DDPr 35/23

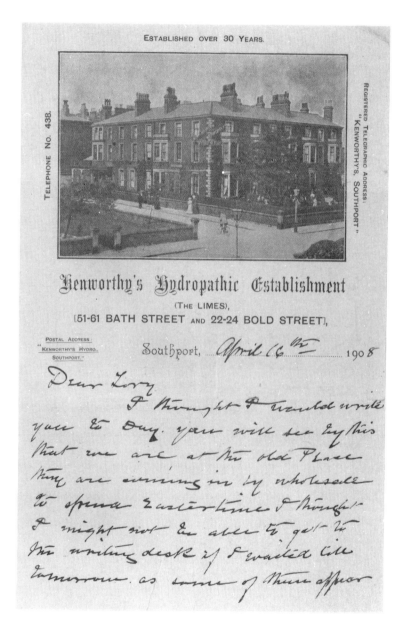

ESTABLISHED OVER 30 YEARS.

TELEPHONE No. 438.

REGISTERED TELEGRAPHIC ADDRESS: "KENWORTHY'S, SOUTHPORT"

Kenworthy's Hydropathic Establishment
(THE LIMES),
[51-61 BATH STREET AND 22-24 BOLD STREET],

POSTAL ADDRESS:
"KENWORTHY'S HYDRO.
SOUTHPORT."

Southport, *April 16* 190 8

This Edwardian letter from Kenworthy's Hydro at Southport suggests that it had a loyal clientele and a busy Easter season.

growth; and on the eve of the railway age their impact in Lancashire was limited. It was still hard to sell land for development in
Southport in the 1820s, and there was no full-scale Assembly
Room for polite society, concerts and balls until 1831. Blackpool's
assemblies still took place in hotels until the Victoria Terrace and
Promenade opened in 1837, and Morecambe (still known as Poul-
ton-le-Sands until the railway re-christened it) had baths, bathing-
machines and a few new 'marine villas' by 1840, but little else
beyond a handful of inns. Compared with the sophistication of the
south coast, where investment in the paraphernalia of the holiday
season had been accumulating over most of the past century, Lancashire's seaside was stunted in its development and rustic in its
amenities. In the mid-1830s the 2,000 visitors who descended on
Blackpool in mid-August filled the little resort to overflowing.

THE RAILWAYS did not so much open out new possibilities as
greatly increase the scope of existing ones in most of the resorts,
although at Morecambe their influence was
arguably more basic and formative. The
story begins with the opening of the Preston   *The Impact of the*
and Wyre railway to Fleetwood in 1840.
This was a speculation by the eccentric so-   *Railways*
cial reformer and visionary Sir Peter
Hesketh–Fleetwood, who wanted to develop
a new port, resort and model community on his land at the Wyre
estuary. For a short time things went well, and Decimus Burton's
classical terraces began to march along the shore, while the North
Euston Hotel was built for passengers in transit to Scotland. But
Sir Peter ran out of money, and Fleetwood's status as the gateway
to Scotland proved only temporary as the railway conquered the
Shap fells. Ironically, Sir Peter had to sell his estates at Blackpool
and Southport in an unavailing attempt to salvage the Fleetwood
scheme; and to compound the irony, the main beneficiaries of his
railway were the rival resorts of Blackpool and Lytham. Blackpool had boomed since the opening of the railway, as horse
omnibuses covered the short distance from Poulton-le-Fylde with
unprecedented convenience; and branch lines were opened,
cheaply, across the Fylde plain to both resorts in 1846.
    This early link between the Fylde resorts and the population
centres was brought about by plans for commercial and long-
distance passenger traffic, rather than through any initial perception

of the opportunities offered by the seaside holiday market; and the same was true of the railway's arrival at Morecambe in 1848. This was part of a commercial port project, in association with the 'little' North Western railway from the West Riding of Yorkshire; and in 1850 the link between Morecambe and Leeds and Bradford was completed. Meanwhile, Southport had been joined to Liverpool by rail in 1848, and in 1855 it acquired a direct link with industrial Lancashire by way of Wigan. Here too, commercial port development was in the minds of the promoters, although it did not come to anything.

It is significant that holiday traffic, highly seasonal as it was, did not offer sufficient attractions in itself for heavy investment in railways to the coast. But the railways did make a considerable impact on resort development. Above all, by cutting costs and times dramatically, they expanded the market for seaside holidays, while their carrying capacity enabled the transport system to cope with increased demand. Middle-class visitors from lower down the social scale than hitherto were able to make the journey, stay longer and spend more. For (at first) an affluent minority with unusual command over their time, the railways also made possible a new lifestyle involving living at the seaside and commuting to work in Liverpool, Manchester or the manufacturing towns, during the summer months or even all the year round. But the new means of transport also made it much easier for large numbers of working-class pleasure-seekers to reach the coast, especially when the scope for organizing cheap excursions became apparent. This soon generated conflict within the resorts, as noisy, boisterous trippers with a well-developed taste for alcohol rubbed shoulders with respectable visitors and affluent residents in the streets and on the beaches. Resorts had to find ways of coping with regular influxes of working-class visitors at week-ends throughout the summer, in much larger numbers than the 'Bathing Sunday' artisans. Some were able to be more successfully discouraging than others, and there were important contrasts between Blackpool and Morecambe, where there were no dominant landowners to control development and sustain what contemporaries called an 'elevated social tone', and Southport and Lytham, where the landed families on whose estates the resorts were largely built were able to defend their status as havens of peace and respectability, with the help of local government bodies whose members shared their priorities.

The railways did not cause these developments on their own: rather, they enabled them to take place, which is important, but not

Sunday Schools and similar organisations continued to organise trips to
the seaside in the late nineteenth and early twentieth century, and this
crowded station platform at Haslingden looks like just such an occasion.

the same thing. There was a significant time-lag between the
opening of the railways to the resorts and the emergence of
working-class holiday demand as a potentially important contribu-
tor to resort economies. That development took place from the
1870s onwards, and working-class custom was channelled
overwhelmingly into Blackpool, and to a lesser extent into
Morecambe.

In the latter case, the policies of the Midland Railway in offering cheap fares from the West Riding of Yorkshire, boosted by advertising campaigns, made a significant difference to the outcome;
but the reasons for Blackpool's remarkable transformation into the
world's first working-class seaside resort must be sought elsewhere, for the railway companies did not favour Blackpool over its
Lancashire rivals, and at times their policies actually held back
development in the short run as they failed to keep pace with
increasing demand.

FROM the 1840s onwards the Lancashire seaside resorts had to learn to live with day-trippers or 'excursionists'. The Liverpool and Manchester Railway had run a Sunday School excursion as early as 1831, and the Preston and Wyre Railway offered very cheap fares during August from its first season in 1840. Each resort in turn was inundated with trippers as soon as the railway reached it: the effects were felt particularly strongly in Southport when the direct line from the cotton towns opened in 1855. Many early trips were organised by Sunday schools or the temperance movement, or even (in Preston, for example) by committees of local philanthropists, to encourage working-class people to seek healthy, 'rational' recreations away from the smoke and moral contamination of the manufacturing towns.

Trippers and Holidaymakers

Such excursions were promoted with particular eagerness at times of fair and festivity inland, with a view to distracting workers, and especially children, from the attendant drunkenness, gambling and immorality. Employers also organised cheap trips for their workpeople, in the hope of building good industrial relations by promoting a sense of loyalty to the firm and the family, often as part of a wider strategy of industrial paternalism. Many of the early excursions were to some extent policed by the organisers, although complaints of drunken trippers on Sunday School or even temperance excursions suggest that the need to sell tickets sometimes prevented close investigation of the lifestyles of the purchasers.

From the beginning, trips like this were supplemented by the regular offerings of the railway companies themselves, and by the purely commercial activities of excursion agents. Increasingly, groups of workpeople also began to organise their own trips. Such excursions were more suspect in the eyes of the self-consciously respectable among the established residents and visitors, especially when they took place on Sundays, when they were particularly attractive to the thirsty and uninhibited. The Clifton family, lords of the manor of Lytham, were able to suppress the Sunday excursions to their resort by lobbying the railway company; but the defenders of Blackpool's Sabbath peace were less influential, and the crowds of 'shoeblacks and barbers' apprentices', as they were angrily described in 1849, continued to scandalize their 'betters' until the Sunday trips were withdrawn in 1856.

This unusual attachment to Sunday excursions was sympto-
matic of a more general enthusiasm for cheap trips on the part of
the Lancashire and Yorkshire Railway in these early years; and in
the early 1850s Blackpool might play host to as many as 12,000
working-class visitors during an August week-end. This strained
facilities of all kinds to the limit, and special arrangements had to
be made to cope with the influx. Already, working-class visitors
were using cheap four-day tickets to stay beyond the week-end;
and the popular season developed steadily alongside the middle-
class holidaymakers, who were beginning to colonise quieter areas
to the north and south of the original resort centre. This pattern of
development was much more strongly in evidence at Blackpool
than anywhere else on the Lancashire coast in the 1850s and 1860s,
although Southport (after 1855) and Morecambe were also taking a
share of the working-class market.

But it was from the 1870s onwards that the floodgates really
opened, in spite of increasingly restrictive railway policies on fares
and cheap ticket arrangements; and it was then that Blackpool really established its pioneering working-class image and identity.
As well as day-trips and week-ends, working-class people from the
cotton towns began to stay from Saturday night until the Wednes-
day of the following week; and by the 1880s and 1890s holidays
were lengthening to a whole week, although for families from a
few places, such as Bolton and Rochdale, this process took a little
longer. By the early twentieth century some towns were adding a
short September break to the main holiday, and the popular season
began to lengthen. From the 1880s onwards, too, Blackpool began
to expand its catchment area for working-class visitors, reaching
beyond Lancashire and the West Riding to draw in customers first
from Birmingham and the West Midlands, then from Nottingham,
the East Midlands and even further afield. In 1873 about 850,000
passengers arrived at Blackpool's railway stations during the season. By 1883 there were more than 1,300,000 arrivals, and in 1903
nearly three million. By the eve of the First World War the four
million mark was fast approaching. Growth of visitor numbers on
this scale was uniquely a Blackpool phenomenon, and it continued
during the inter-war years. The town's publicists claimed seven
million visitors per year during the 1930s, far in excess of any of
the competition. Within Lancashire, only Morecambe travelled any
distance down this road: Lytham put the shutters up on working-
class visitors at mid-century, and Southport had very much followed suit by the 1870s. Morecambe's railway links with Leeds

and Bradford made it particularly dependent on the West Yorkshire textile districts, and it became known as 'Bradford-by-sea'. The rail route from cotton Lancashire was roundabout, even when a line was built to link Blackburn with Hellifield and the Leeds–Morecambe route in 1880; and in 1894 an intrepid seasonal commuter to Rochdale could not arrive at work until 11.15 a.m. The Yorkshire traffic was subject to competition from Blackpool itself, as well as from Scarborough and other east coast resorts; and wages were lower and holidays shorter in the West Riding. Even so, Morecambe advanced jauntily during the 1880s and 1890s; but even in 1894 it attracted fewer than 8,000 visitors from Leeds and Bradford put together on August Bank Holiday Monday, at a time when Blackpool's total visitor numbers for this peak week-end would be at least ten times that number. And when the enduring slump in the West Riding textile trades deepened into crisis at the turn of the century, Morecambe's development lurched to a halt, to be revived only in the inter-war years. Blackpool continued on its merry way. Clearly, what most needs explaining on the Lancashire coast is the rise of Blackpool, especially in the crucial formative and transitional years between the early 1870s and 1914.

Certain distinctive characteristics of the Lancashire cotton towns were essential to Blackpool's rise. Family incomes at working-class levels were unusually high and reliable by the 1870s, with a relatively high proportion of skilled and supervisory occupations for men and comparatively good male wages in all jobs, coupled with the area's uniquely high demand for female and child labour, which was again relatively well-paid, especially for adolescents and in weaving. The price fall of the late nineteenth century helped these incomes to go further and released money to be spent on consumer durables, clothes and leisure. People from the cotton towns worked hard, but they also played and consumed enthusiastically. Interruptions to their work became fewer, too, whether in the form of casual holidays, trade disputes or lay-offs due to depression: this pioneer industrial society was learning to produce in a sustained and disciplined way with a minimum of conflict and disruption. Working-class thrift, saving and mutual assistance organizations like the Friendly Societies and the Co-op were also thick on the ground, and this made it easier to save for a desired goal. The seaside holiday soon fell into this category, as people worked and saved steadily through the year, increasingly putting their money into special

Even after the main Blackpool railway stations were greatly expanded at the turn of the century, the crush at the height of the season could be frightening. Here is Central Station on 19 August 1916. War or no war, it was 'business as usual' at this point.

neighbourhood-based holiday savings clubs, in order to enjoy a 'fifty-second week' of enjoyment at the seaside.

THE SEASIDE was only one outlet for this hard-earned leisure spending, but it became a very important one. This was partly due to the distinctive local holiday system. The traditional holidays at Whitsuntide and the local wakes and fairs had survived the coming of the factory system, as popular attachment to them outweighed the pressure for labour discipline; and during the second half of the nineteenth century they were extended and transformed. In the early railway age the trains brought

The making of the

Wakes weeks

Blackpool's Promenade in 1890, looking towards the North Pier. The
Tower was still a thing of the future, and the long front gardens of the
houses on South Beach had not yet acquired the stalls and roundabouts
which were to become controversial later in the decade.

additional people to the local festivities in the major centres, while
providing opportunities for excursions to the seaside and country-
side which were enjoyed in addition to the customary local plea-
sures. Increasingly, however, people began to go away for the
whole wakes, and to stay away for an extra day or two if times
were good. The employers made the best of this, and tolerated the
absences, using the week's closure, as it became, for whitewash-
ing and renovation. By the 1870s some of the wakes fairground
amusements were migrating to the coast, and by the 1890s some
cotton towns had a deserted air at holiday time. The local newspapers for the holidaymaking towns were sold at the seaside, and
those who stayed behind were a disadvantaged minority of the
poorly-paid, the families with children too young to work, and the
elderly. Going away to the seaside became almost the norm in the
gossipy, tightly-knit neighbourhoods of third-generation industrial families, and this in turn helped to spread the practice further.

No other industrial area developed the seaside holiday habit as early or as thoroughly as this, and even within Lancashire the mining and heavy industry centres around Wigan and St Helens did not follow the same path. Moreover, the way in which the 'Bathing Sunday' tradition transferred itself to the wakes ensured that a full-scale working-class holiday season could develop, as working-class holidaymakers were heading for the coast in significant numbers throughout the summer months between Burnley fair in early July and Oldham wakes in early September, as each town enjoyed its own distinctive holidays. This was in marked contrast to those areas of the country in which working-class seaside visits were concentrated into August Bank Holiday week, after the introduction of this new national holiday in 1871; and in cotton Lancashire, as in the West Riding of Yorkshire and other industrial areas where old summer holidays had survived, August Bank Holiday was unnecessary and unimportant.

BUT WHY was Blackpool, in particular, the dominant attraction for the working-class holidaymakers of the cotton towns? As I have suggested, the railways were not the only answer. Blackpool had a head start over Southport, in particular, because of the earliness of its rail connection with inland Lancashire; but during the last thirty years of the nineteenth century its main feeder line, the Lancashire and Yorkshire Railway, was inefficient, tardy and unwilling to encourage traffic by offering competitive tourist and excursion tickets. Despite the enormous growth in the Blackpool traffic, it failed to improve terminal facilities until the turn of the century, and non-corridor trains sometimes took 2½ hours to cover the twenty miles or so between Preston and Blackpool. By the early twentieth century the L & Y was keeping pace with Blackpool's growth, but it had not actively encouraged it. The most important reasons for the channelling of working-class holiday demand into Blackpool lay in the peculiar characteristics of the town itself. These in turn enabled Blackpool to become so popular that the fame of its attractions became in itself a stimulus to further growth in the popular holiday industry.

Blackpool: its character and development

In the first place, Blackpool's pattern of landownership was an important influence. It was divided among a large number of small freeholders, and the more substantial, and strategically-placed, block of sea-front land belonging to Sir Peter Hesketh–Fleetwood was sold off with minimal building restrictions to small speculators in the early 1840s. This sub-division of property worked against planning or development on the grand scale. Developers built whatever would sell quickly or bring in a reliable return; and owners had no incentive to impose minimum standards, especially after the visiting public was opened out and democratized by the railway in the 1840s. Where there was a consensus among developers that the high-class market was also the better-paying, as at Windermere or Grange-over-Sands, land sub-division could be compatible with a high social tone; but this was not the case in Blackpool. Houses were packed on to small plots of land, with unpretentious brick and stucco frontages and the minimum of space at the back. Any individual who attempted to go significantly up-market was vulnerable to his neighbours, who might sabotage his efforts by putting slums or pigsties next door. The Cliftons of Lytham, recognising the situation, gave up their original plan to build semi-detached villas with planned gardens on their perfectly-sited Blackpool estate between what is now North Station and the sea,

Southport eventually turned the retreat of the sea to its advantage, as the Corporation invested in entertainments and amenities on the foreshore, as this view of King's Garden and Marine Lake in the 1920s shows.

and joined the scramble to build poky little terraces of the standard type. This set the pattern for the rest of the Victorian years.

This lack of architectural formality and dignity would have set narrow limits to Blackpool's potential for growth as a 'better-class' resort, especially as its only (though not negligible) natural assets were a long sandy beach and a boisterous sea which came right up to the promenade. Southport and Lytham had plenty of sand but saw too little of the sea, which began to retreat in earnest from Southport in the late nineteenth century. 'The sea saw Southport and fled', said one Blackpool wag. Morecambe on the other hand, was perpetually lacking in sand, and visited only occasionally by the sea, while its proximity to attractive scenery was considered to be a disadvantage by some locals, as it took visitors and their money out of town for too long. Blackpool lacked even this double-edged advantage, and its deficiencies in both natural endowment and architecture and planning helped to ensure that, within Lancashire, Southport would take the lion's share of the 'better-class' trade which paid best for most of the nineteenth century.

Under normal circumstances Blackpool's shortcomings as a 'better-class' resort would have stunted its growth and condemned it to obscurity. Under Lancashire conditions, however, disadvantages turned to opportunities. Blackpool's unpretentious architecture and layout were attractive to working-class visitors who found the similarities with their accustomed surroundings reassuring, even to the sett-paved central streets; and the lack of building controls extended to the use that was made of buildings and gardens after development. Public houses proliferated and flourished, and front gardens were turned over to oyster stalls, steam roundabouts, fortune telling, character reading and other catchpenny amusements, wherever the crowds gathered. Blackpool was similarly hospitable to the fish and chip trade from the 1880s onwards, and the lack of a dominant and restrictive lord of the manor with powers over the foreshore made it easier for a full-scale fairground to establish itself on the beach. All this informality and free and easy enjoyment was well calculated to appeal to the new working-class market of the later nineteenth century; and the stance adopted by local government added to the encouragement.

Blackpool's local authority had tremendous scope for influencing the resort's development, as a provider of amenities and services and as a regulator of standards and public behaviour. In the first place, it was, in a town of divided landownership, the only possible source of finance and planning for a promenade and sea defences. It was the successful completion of a sea-front promenade in 1870, at what was then the enormous cost for a small town of £60,000, that first gave the Local Board of Health the confidence to undertake large projects, and the ratepayers the trust in the future to support them. The boom years which followed the construction of the promenade showed the local citizenry that collective investment in amenities could give them a competitive edge over rival resorts; and this lesson was not forgotten. It made it easier for the municipality to obtain support for further expensive schemes of promenade extension and widening in the late nineteenth and early twentieth century, to protect the northern part of the town from erosion and then simply to make room for the enormous growth in visitor numbers. This was done under the auspices

Smalley's company-house in Blackpool advertises its proprietor's roots in Lostock Hall, and this photograph features a party of visitors from his home town, where he had been an ice-cream vendor before moving to Blackpool.

Kiosks and advertising slogans were already present in profusion on Blackpool's Central Pier by 1880, when dancing of a heavy-footed and uninhibited kind had already become an established attraction.

of the borough corporation which took over from the Local Board in 1876, and which played a crucially important part in helping the town to adjust successfully to the working-class influx on which its future depended.

Between 1876 and 1914, and especially in the late nineteenth century, the Corporation was dominated by leading members of the business community, with interests in the holiday industry, drink, and the building trades. Convivial cliques of entertainment entrepreneurs, property developers and publicans, led by people like W.H. Cocker of the Aquarium and Winter Gardens, and later the Bickerstaffe brothers of the Tower, Steamboat Company and Central Pier, with their fingers in several pies, effectively ran the town in their own interests, which coincided with those of the popular holiday industry. This showed itself most obviously in the Corporation's advertising policy. Blackpool was unique among Victorian and Edwardian seaside resorts in obtaining, in 1879, the power to devote the proceeds of a rate of two old pence in the pound to advertising the town's attractions. Other resorts were denied permission to do this, and the reasons for Blackpool's exceptional

*Blackpool's autumn illuminations developed on a remarkable scale
during the inter-war years, providing a successful solution to the problem
shared by most seaside resorts of how to extend the short summer season.*

status are shrouded in mystery. Right from the start, the Advertising Committee invested in the popular season. It concentrated on
the most democratic form of advertising, the picture poster dis-
played at railway stations, and extended its coverage into the Midlands and then further afield, combining new poster initiatives with
special excursion deals with the railway companies. Only when the
working-class season was thoroughly established at the turn of the
century, and more money became available for advertising, did the
Corporation revive an earlier policy of offering fêtes and special
attractions to extend the season for a 'better-class' market; and this
was the policy which produced the famous autumn illuminations
for the first time in 1912.

The autumn illuminations depended heavily on the expertise of
the Corporation's electricity department; and as early as 1879 the
promenade had been electrically lit for the first time. This piece of

pioneering was itself used as a tourist attraction. Meanwhile, and less glamorously, the municipal gasworks generated fat profits to set against local taxation, and when the Corporation took over the running of the tramway in 1892 the joy-riding of summer visitors enabled the network to expand to keep pace with the town's growth in succeeding years. Care was taken over refuse collection and the quality of drainage and water supply, too, although the latter was not directly a Corporation responsibility.

Where attracting, keeping and satisfying visitors were not so obviously an issue, however, the Corporation was more concerned with keeping property taxes low and pacifying the legions of small businesspeople who were made uneasy by high levels of municipal spending. Thus no public park was provided: the beach was thought to be sufficient for visitors, and all offers of land from private donors came with strings attached. Sewage treatment was kept to the minimum necessary to avoid visible pollution of the beach. No public baths were provided for the locals, although they were often promised at election time. A public library was established early, in 1880, when it was thought likely to be an attraction for 'better-class' visitors; but priorities changed, this proved not to be the case, and the library was neglected. Outside the realm of the holiday industry, Blackpool was as parsimonious as any authority whose voters were drawn mainly from small businessmen and owners of house property. It became in the late nineteenth century, to a unique extent, a town of landladies; and a policy of spending to encourage the popular holiday season, while economising on everything else, fitted their priorities very well.

BLACKPOOL's local government had a difficult tightrope to walk when dealing with public order. On the one hand, visitors had to be protected from the importunities of touts and street musicians, and allowed to enjoy themselves unmolested. On the other hand, a *Visitors and* lot of visitors – and not only working-class ones – enjoyed music and alfresco entertain- *Entertainment* ment in the streets and on the beach, and patronised stallholders and street vendors who from a 'respectable' perspective were unsightly and a nuisance, and competed unfairly with established ratepayers. Similarly, there were conflicting attitudes to drink and Sunday observance, for Blackpool was not without a vocal Nonconformist presence, and there remained a vociferous minority of advocates of a policy of respectability, putting advertisements in newspapers rather than on hoardings and re-planning the town centre to retain and expand the middle-class market which had prevailed until the 1870s. But as Blackpool's rulers gained more power over the town's policing, culminating in the setting up of a borough police force in 1887 and a borough magistracy in 1899, so they became less restrictive. They did not allow a free for all. In 1901 the Corporation obtained power to stop the further spread of street and forecourt stalls, which had been expanding rapidly in and around the central area between the North and Central Piers, and especially just to the south of the then Central Station, where most of the excursion trains arrived. Here the Golden Mile of inter-war fame was already emerging, and the local authority was concerned to keep it in its place. Fiercer action involving the suppression of existing stalls was not sanctioned, however; and the Corporation also had to beat a retreat in 1897 when it tried to abolish the fairground which had developed on the beach in the same area. Hundreds of stallholders, from phrenologists and shooting gallery owners to chiropodists and patent medicine vendors, were threatened, and so was the pleasure of large numbers of working-class visitors; but a chorus of disapproval from the popular press of the inland towns forced the Corporation to draw back and use its newly-acquired powers over the beach to regulate the fairground and charge rent for pitches, but not to suppress it.

Intervention of this kind was unusual in Blackpool, and there were those who thought that the big entertainment interests who were well represented in the Town Hall might have resented the showmen's competition. Similar things were said a few years later when unavailing attempts were made to hamstring the infant Pleasure Beach, a fairground among sand dunes at the south end of the promenade, by imposing strict conditions on its operations; but here there was also opposition from established residents who saw the tranquillity and respectability of their neat semi-detached houses under threat from hordes of pleasure-seeking day-trippers.

In general, however, the enjoyments of the visitors and those who ministered to them were lightly policed. Nude bathing could not be tolerated, and the foreshore inspector was issued with a telescope to check on offenders at low tide. But the drunkenness statistics were remarkably low for a resort to which working-class men went for a binge in huge numbers, and police and magistrates were clearly tolerant of harmless boisterousness. Moreover, and

Blackpool Pleasure Beach in 1910, when it was really beginning to develop on a large scale. In the centre is the Sir Hiram Maxim Captive Flying Machine. A few years earlier this site beyond the southern end of the promenade and its tramway had been sand-dunes, with gipsy fortune-tellers looking for whatever custom might come their way.

especially from the 1890s, Blackpool's attitude to Sunday observance was uniquely permissive, symbolised by the introduction of Sunday trams in 1896, which was denounced by a Primitive Methodist minister as showing Blackpool to be more immoral that Paris or Sodom. Very different attitudes prevailed in Southport, and in towns like Bolton in Blackpool's hinterland; but most visitors seem to have put away their inhibitions about Sunday pleasure, and perhaps about other things too, as they got off the train. Perhaps the most telling example of Corporation non-intervention, however, was the enforcement of minimum building by-laws: during a period of several years in the late nineteenth century when the decisions of the Building Plans Committee were monitored, most of the approved plans broke the official building by-laws, usually in the interests of packing more bedrooms, and therefore more rent and income, on to a given plot of land. This helped to ensure the supply of cheap accommodation which was another ingredient in the Blackpool success story; and the costs in terms of health and discomfort were less calculable than the profits.

What Blackpool Corporation did not need to do was invest in the entertainment industry. In contrast to many resorts, including well-known popular centres such as Margate, private enterprise was able to keep pace with demand, and indeed to stimulate it, without the need for local government intervention or support. Development began in earnest in the 1860s and proceeded on an impressive scale in the following decade, as the popular season took off. After a short hiatus following the depression of 1879, investment resumed on an altogether novel scale in the 1890s, and by the turn of the century Blackpool's entertainment industry had far outpaced all its seaside competitors, within and beyond Lancashire.

The 1860s were pier-building years in England and Wales generally, and Blackpool was no exception. The North Pier opened

The classic view of Blackpool beach at the turn of the century, with the Tower and Gigantic Wheel presiding over a crowded beach, and pleasure boats doing a brisk trade alongside the bathing machines.

in 1863 as a basic promenade pier and steamer jetty, with no provision for entertainments. It slotted in alongside other investment in middle-class amenities during the decade. But the second pier, the South Jetty, was very different. Later to become the Central Pier, its purpose was to lure excursionists away from the North Pier, where their presence was annoying 'respectable' visitors, and from 1870 onwards it made fat profits by offering dancing and cheap steamer trips, with a growing variety of side-shows. On the same basis, the Raikes Hall pleasure gardens offered the tripper dancing, fireworks, acrobats and alcohol, with an unofficial admixture of prostitution, and this formula was successful until the advent of rivals closer to the sea front in the 1890s. Meanwhile, however, the promoters of the Winter Gardens in 1875 at first looked to the 'better-class' market, offering an all-weather promenade and up-market concerts, and hoping to stimulate a winter season. This did not work, and from the mid-1880s the Winter Gardens followed Raikes Hall inexorably down-market, offering music-hall and such delights as a female human cannonball under the management of William Holland, a fly and extrovert self-publicist recruited from London music-hall.

The transition to popular amusement on the grand scale was completed in the 1890s. It was then that Blackpool acquired its enduring emblem, the Tower, and two years later a second accent on the skyline, the Gigantic Wheel, opened in 1896. At the turn of the century a further pleasure palace, the Alhambra, opened next door to the Tower, and well over half a million pounds had been invested in entertainment complexes on Blackpool's sea-front during the decade. The subsequent development of the Pleasure Beach at the south end of the promenade, from gipsy encampment to sophisticated funfair displaying all the latest American electrical technology, was further icing on an already rich cake. The Tower, Alhambra and Winter Gardens could each provide all-weather entertainment of all kinds for a sixpenny entrance fee, with everything from ballrooms and music-hall to exhibitions, circuses and zoos. There was nothing to approach the magnitude of this in Europe, and only New York's Coney Island (essentially a day-tripper resort) and possibly Atlantic City could rival it in the world.

As the scale of the entertainment industry grew, it attracted investment from further afield. The early promotions brought together local and Lancashire entrepreneurs, with a lot of drive coming from members of old Blackpool yeoman families who had done well out of land and building speculations and accumulated

money to invest. By the 1890s London and Home Counties speculators were becoming interested in the big schemes; but in the case
of the Tower this interest lay partly in making a killing out of semi-
fraudulent property speculation, and it took a local boy made good,
John Bickerstaffe, to rescue the scheme from these malefactors and
help it to succeed. The Alhambra, too, was financially unsound,
and had to be taken over and rescued by the Tower Company. What
is clear, however, is that Blackpool's big entertainment companies
were not only more numerous, but also more successful, than their
counterparts elsewhere; and there was no shortage of demand for
what they had to offer.

By the 1880s and 1890s Blackpool's entertainment complexes
were becoming sufficiently famous and attractive to be making
their own contribution to explaining the resort's growth. People
chose Blackpool because it had an incomparable range of attractions geared up to working-class tastes: or at least, to the tastes of
the overwhelming majority. Alongside the pleasure palaces, of
course, there were also theatres, music-halls, waxworks, fairground
amusements, and pubs, all in a setting which combined reassuring
familiarity (brick terraced houses and the presence of friends and
neighbours) with a sense of release, binge, tolerance and vulgar
fun. Everything was larger than life, but not deterringly remote
from it.

Blackpool made its fortune from specialising in working-class
visitors from an ever-widening catchment area; but another of its
strengths was that it was able to retain a substantial middle-class
presence. The sea-front north of the North Pier had been developed
to a higher standard, and protected from noise and unseemliness,
by a Land Company; and the Corporation was much more vigilant
in protecting the amenities of this area than it was in the town
centre. At the other end of the sea-front, too, a quieter style of holidaymaking prevailed; and the amusements of the town centre did
not exclude the more tolerant and adventurous of the Edwardian
middle classes, especially as the trippers themselves became more
'civilised' and disciplined in their behaviour. By the turn of the century commuters, commercial travellers and retired residents were
becoming important elements in the Blackpool population; and this
theme became much more pronounced in the inter-war years. Not
all even of the mid-Victorian middle classes were staid, decorous
and ultra-respectable, especially when they got away from the
tyranny of the neighbours; and Blackpool attracted plenty of the
cheerful pleasure-seekers among the middle classes. Ultimately, in

fact, by cultivating such a distinctive identity it may well have attracted more middle-class patrons than it otherwise might.

BUT the most successful middle-class resort of Lancashire was
Southport, which took a very different course. It outpaced its
rivals comfortably for most of the nineteenth
century, doing particularly well between
mid-century and the First World War. The
influence of large landed estates was crucial
to its destiny. The land on which Southport
was built belonged almost entirely to two
families, just as the adjoining resort of

Southport:

middle-class haven

Birkdale was owned by the Weld-Blundells. This made a high
standard of development possible, indeed likely: large landed
estates were able to plan on the grand scale and to look to the
future, especially when they let development land on 99-year
leases which would eventually revert to the estate. Some aristo-
cratic developers also preferred to house the comfortably-off in
appropriate style, especially when they themselves lived close
by: it was in tune with their own status and aesthetic preferences.
But there was more to the rise of Southport than this simple
formula.

The bathing season at Southport had originated in the visits of
the Bold family, one of the dominant landowners. But development
was piecemeal, sporadic and almost unsupervised, making very
little money for the landlords, until the early 1840s. But in 1842-
3, just before the coming of the railway, both of the big estates
changed hands. The part owned by Sir Peter Hesketh Fleetwood,
the obsessive developer of Fleetwood to the north of Blackpool,
was sold to his brother, Rev. Charles Hesketh, the rector of the
parish. Meanwhile, Charles Scarisbrick bought up the other
great estate from the financially embarrassed Sir Henry Bold-
Hoghton. Charles Hesketh was cautious, staunchly and restric-
tively Evangelical in his religious outlook, and determined not
to speculate rashly as his brother had done. Charles Scarisbrick
was aggressively entrepreneurial, determined to maximise the income from everything he did, entirely devoid of public spirit, and
anxious to use the revenue from development at Southport to provide for his three illegitimate children. He had already made a fortune in property speculation in Paris, and he knew a good
opportunity when he saw one. The policies of these unusual and

Lord Street, Southport's central boulevard and most prestigious shopping street. It owes its spacious layout more to an accident of topography than to any insight on the part of the landowners, but its value to the resort has been immense. Notice the invalid in the bath-chair, heading out of the picture to the right.

utterly dissimilar men were remarkably complementary. As Southport developed under their auspices, it was almost as if Hesketh provided the dominant moral tone of restrictive respectability, while Scarisbrick provided the dynamism and entrepreneurial spirit which were the engines of growth.

Southport's landowners did not share the enthusiasm of their contemporaries in other resorts for boosting growth by donating land and amenities for public purposes. Nor did they make many concessions to developers, who were expected to make up their own roads and provide their own sewers. When Charles Hesketh donated the land for Hesketh Park in 1865 he required the local authority to lay out the surrounding area, which he still owned, as a high-class building estate, and did very well out of the transaction. He did have a high profile in Southport charities, unlike Charles Scarisbrick and the trustees who took over the management of his estate on his death in 1860. Both estates insisted on

Southport's Winter Gardens as originally envisaged at their opening in 1874, with the accent on formal walks and improving recreations for polite society.

large plots, high minimum house values, and strict building and use controls because they seemed likely to pay best, not out of any sense of philanthropy. They were often willing to remove covenants in exchange for a money payment when it suited them. Southport's pretensions to being a 'Garden City' resort owe at least as much to the tree-planting and street-improving activities of local government as to its landowning families.

To some degree, of course, the landowners constructed a local elite in their own preferred image. The Improvement Commission, and the Corporation which took over in 1867, were dominated by wealthy retired businessmen and substantial local traders who were anxious to sustain the tranquillity of their chosen town. So they eagerly endorsed Charles Hesketh's early Victorian restraints on entertainment, as the horse races and regatta were proscribed, the theatre discouraged and Sunday amusements prohibited. Nor were they at all happy about an expansion of drink facilities for the working-class visitors who swarmed into Southport after the opening of the new railway in 1855. Besides, Liverpool's 'roughs' were too close for comfort. Even the mainstream visiting public of respectable tradesmen and shopkeepers was viewed askance. As in Blackpool, the 1870s were crucial. Following on from their successful promotion of the very long pier, which opened in 1860, local business interests invested in a range of public buildings and entertainment facilities which aimed at the 'respectable' middle-class market. And the philanthropic activities of the 'retired cotton princes', as John Liddle called them, provided a library, an art gallery, an observatory and a string of elegant and opulent churches of several denominations. Meanwhile, the working-class trippers were discouraged with deepening severity. The upshot was that while the 1870s saw Blackpool change course almost irrevocably in a working-class direction, Southport's popular holiday season collapsed (aided by a well-publicised smallpox outbreak) and instead it experienced unparalleled growth as a residential centre. The paths of the two resorts had diverged, and Southport's future was to be dominated by comfortably-off commuters and retired residents, mainly of a Nonconformist or otherwise serious-minded Evangelical cast of mind. This contrasted with Blackpool, whose civic leaders and well-off residents were much more likely to be religiously indifferent or nominal Anglicans, and Conservative in politics as opposed to Southport's predominant Liberalism. Politically, in fact, Southport's landowners had conjured up a local elite with diametrically opposed views to their own authoritarian Conservative attitudes; but although this led to fierce conflict over who should hold power in the resort, it did not materially affect what kind of resort Southport became.

Just as Blackpool never became entirely a trippers' paradise, so Southport never gave up completely on catering for holiday-makers. As the sea retreated in the late nineteenth century, the Corporation invested in marine lakes and gardens, after a monumental battle with the landowners over who should control the foreshore. There was even a fairground which shared some of the Pleasure Beach's attractions. But the contrast in style and substance is nevertheless arresting.

THE other important Lancashire resorts likewise fell on either side of the divide between working-class and middle-class, and to some extent the related one between 'rough' and 'respectable'. The twin resorts of Lytham and St Annes are relatively easy to cate- *Lytham, St Annes and* gorise. Lytham grew up under the auspices of a well-established landed family, whose *Morecambe* policies owed much to its hereditary land agents. The Cliftons and Fairs tightened up their controls over the estate as the railways approached, and the 1840s saw carefully-planned leasehold development for a middle-class visitor and residential market, which was sustained thereafter. St Annes also grew up on Clifton land, but it was promoted by a Rossendale syndicate which was looking for better profits than coal or cotton could provide in the later 1870s, and after early difficulties it prospered among the sand-dunes in the late nineteenth and early twentieth century. These resorts perhaps appealed

St Annes, planned by a land syndicate for a late Victorian middle-class market, displays all the spacious hallmarks of Edwardian respectability in the sea-front gardens which had taken the place of the original wilderness of sand-dunes.

The pier at St Anne's followed the fashion for embellishment with elaborate pavilions at the turn of the century. Like many others, it adopted the Oriental style of seaside architecture which went back to the Prince Regent's Pavilion at Brighton a century earlier.

Morecambe's Central Pier in 1872, three years after its opening. It was still a promenade pier and landing stage, without embellishment, but it already had a colourful past, for it had been bought second-hand in 1869, having been intended for Valparaiso in Chile.

Morecambe was still flourishing as a popular resort when this view of the central promenade, looking northwards, was taken in about 1960.

to further strands within the Victorian and Edwardian middle-classes. They emphasised quiet family holidays in a way that neither Blackpool nor Southport did, but at the same time they attracted golfers to their testing courses among the sandhills (an attraction which they shared with Birkdale) and the proximity of Blackpool made other kinds of entertainment accessible. It is interesting to speculate on why Southport did better than Lytham St Annes as a residential resort, but proximity to Liverpool and the advantages of an early start must play an important part in the answer.

Morecambe is less anomalous. The sub-division of a key building estate when the railway arrived at mid-century, and the eagerness of the Midland Railway to generate revenue by offering cheap fares from the West Riding, ensured that it would take the popular path; and this choice was perhaps forced upon it at an earlier stage than Blackpool. In the last quarter of the nineteenth century local and West Riding investors made an impressive effort to build a popular commercial season, with Winter Gardens, Summer Gardens and Tower as well as two piers and an impressive menu of steamer excursions. But there were limits to the scope for Morecambe's growth. It depended too heavily on its Yorkshire

*One of the key changes of the inter-war years was the growing
importance of road transport to the Lancashire seaside resorts. Here a
fleet of charabancs is ready to take a large party of trippers from
Haslingden to an unknown destination.*

catchment area, where the seaside holiday remained the preserve of
a skilled and privileged minority among the workforce until the
inter-war years, when Morecambe came into its own. It was unable
to follow Blackpool in tapping Midland and more distant markets
on a large scale, too, and much of Lancashire itself was out of
reach. It did benefit, along with Blackpool, when the Glasgow and
other Scottish industrial holiday traffic was diverted away from the
Isle of Man during the First World War, and the Lancashire resorts
became lasting beneficiaries of a change of habit. But even in its
heyday in the 1950s, when it benefited from the greater flexibility
of road transport, it remained 'the Yorkshireman's Blackpool', and
continued to live in the shadow of its southern rival. Only since the
1970s has it really become the depressed poor relation among the
Lancashire resorts; but it never assembled the magic cocktail of
ingredients which enabled Blackpool to pioneer a new kind of holiday industry, and gave it a significance of world importance which
is still insufficiently recognised.

THE SEASIDE RESORTS of Lancashire were created and confirmed in enduring images in the half-century or so before the First World War. Fittingly, this is the period which has attracted most of the sustained, in-depth historical research. More needs to be done on the years since 1914. How, exactly, did the World Wars affect the Lancashire resorts?

Epilogue

How did they weather the industrial depressions of the inter-war years, with growing crowds of visitors and expanding populations of commuters and retired residents? How genuinely successful were the holiday seasons of the 1950s (especially) and the 1960s, and why did Blackpool make the transition to the age of the motorway, the package tour, the television and the teenager so much more convincingly than its rivals? What difference to resort policies and amenities did the changing balance between holiday and residential interests bring about? And what about the holiday-makers themselves? What did they expect from their holidays, and did those expectations change? At the moment we have a few clues, especially from the valuable and entertaining surveys of the Blackpool holiday season by Mass-Observation in the late 1930s; but a lot of work will be needed before we can answer any of these questions with confidence. We also need to know more about the social problems of resorts, which are in the public eye now, but which go back a long way in many respects. Seaside labour forces, in seasonal economies dominated by casual labour, insecurity and competition for jobs, have not been able to protect their interests by forming effective trade unions. Local governments have been more concerned with looking after visitors than residents, especially working-class ones, and with keeping local taxation levels as low as possible to attract the comfortably-off. Poverty, indeed, has been endemic at the seaside. Seaside pollution has long been an issue, too: Blackpool's mussels were convicted of causing food poisoning at the turn of the century. All these themes invite research, and I hope that this pamphlet will encourage people to make some contributions of their own.

Bibliography

General background reading on the English seaside

J. A. R. Pimlott, *The Englishman's Holiday: a Social History* (Faber, 1947; reprinted Hassocks, 1976). The pioneering work, and still very useful.

J. K. Walton, *The English Seaside Resort: a Social History, 1750–1914* (Leicester U.P., 1983). A thematic survey with quite a lot of Lancashire material.

J. Walvin, *Beside the Seaside* (Allen Lane, 1978). Still the best introduction to the post-First World War years.

Useful published works on the Lancashire seaside

F. A. Bailey, *A History of Southport* (Angus Downie, 1955). Perhaps a little old-fashioned, but easy and interesting reading.

R. Bingham, *Lost Resort? The Flow and Ebb of Morecambe* (Cicerone, 1990). Contains a lot of interesting newspaper material, but does not use any of the other sources cited here.

Gary Cross (ed.), *Worktowners at Blackpool* (Routledge, 1990). Makes available some fascinating material from the Mass-Observation surveys of the late 1930s.

J. Liddle, 'Estate management and land reform politics: the Hesketh and Scarisbrick families and the making of Southport, 1842 to 1914', in D. Cannadine (ed.),

Patricians, Power and Politics in Nineteenth-Century Towns (Leicester U.P., 1982). Easily the best analysis of Southport's development.

B. Palmer and S. Turner, *The Blackpool Story* (Cleveleys, Authors, 1976). A lively and likeable read.

H. J. Perkin, 'The "social tone" of Victorian seaside resorts in the north west', *Northern History* xi (1976), 180–94. An interesting argument drawn from Lancaster University theses, but containing some factual errors.

J. K. Walton, *The Blackpool Landlady: a Social History* (Manchester U.P., 1978). A social history of Blackpool and its accommodation industry, running through to the 1970s.

J. K. Walton, 'The demand for working-class seaside holidays in Victorian England', *Economic History Review* 34 (1981), 249–65. Contains a lot of Lancashire material.

J. K. Walton, 'Municipal government and the holiday industry in Blackpool, 1876–1914', in J. K. Walton and J. Walvin (eds.), *Leisure in Britain 1780–1939* (Manchester U.P., 1983).

J. K. Walton, 'Railways and resort development in north-west England, 1830–1914', in E. M. Sigsworth (ed.), *Ports and Resorts in the Regions* (School of Humanities and Community Educ., Hull College of Higher

Education, 1980). Includes Cumbria as well as Lancashire.

Theses and dissertations in Lancaster University Library

N. Essafi, 'Some aspects of poverty in Blackpool, 1945–60', M.A., 1990.

J. Gill, 'The origins and development of Grange-over-Sands as a watering-place', M.A., 1969.

J. Grass, 'Morecambe, the people's pleasure. The development of a holiday resort, 1880–1902', M.A., 1972.

M. E. Hutchinson, 'The catering for holiday makers in Fleetwood, 1840–1973', M.A., 1973.

P. Peers, 'The development of St Annes-on-the-Sea as a residential town and watering-place, 1874–1914', M.A., 1979.

G. Rogers, 'Social and economic change on Lancashire landed estates during the nineteenth century, with special reference to the Clifton estate, 1832–1916', Ph.D., 1981. Contains a chapter on Lytham as a resort.

J. K. Walton, 'The social development of Blackpool, 1788–1914', Ph.D., 1974. A lot of material in this does not appear elsewhere.

C. J. Widdowfield, 'The Local Board of Health of Poulton, Bare and Torrisholme and the development of Morecambe, 1852–94', M.A., 1973.

K. R. Wilson, 'Social leaders and public figures in the rise of Morecambe, 1880–1914', M.A., 1972.

I have left out a large number of slight or ephemeral works, concentrating on those which make a real contribution to understanding the development of the Lancashire seaside. There is plenty of room for further work, especially on the twentieth century. Those who want to take up the opportunities will find that the footnotes and bibliographies of the works cited above will lead them into an enormous range of fascinating source material, from newspapers and guide-books to local government and census records, and even to company records and government reports in the Public Record Office at Kew. I should be happy to answer serious enquiries from people who are thinking about starting work in this area.